IMMANUEL LUTHERAN SCHO
W9-CLJ-786

LET'S EXPLORE AMERICA
CALIFORNIA

California

Valerie Bodden

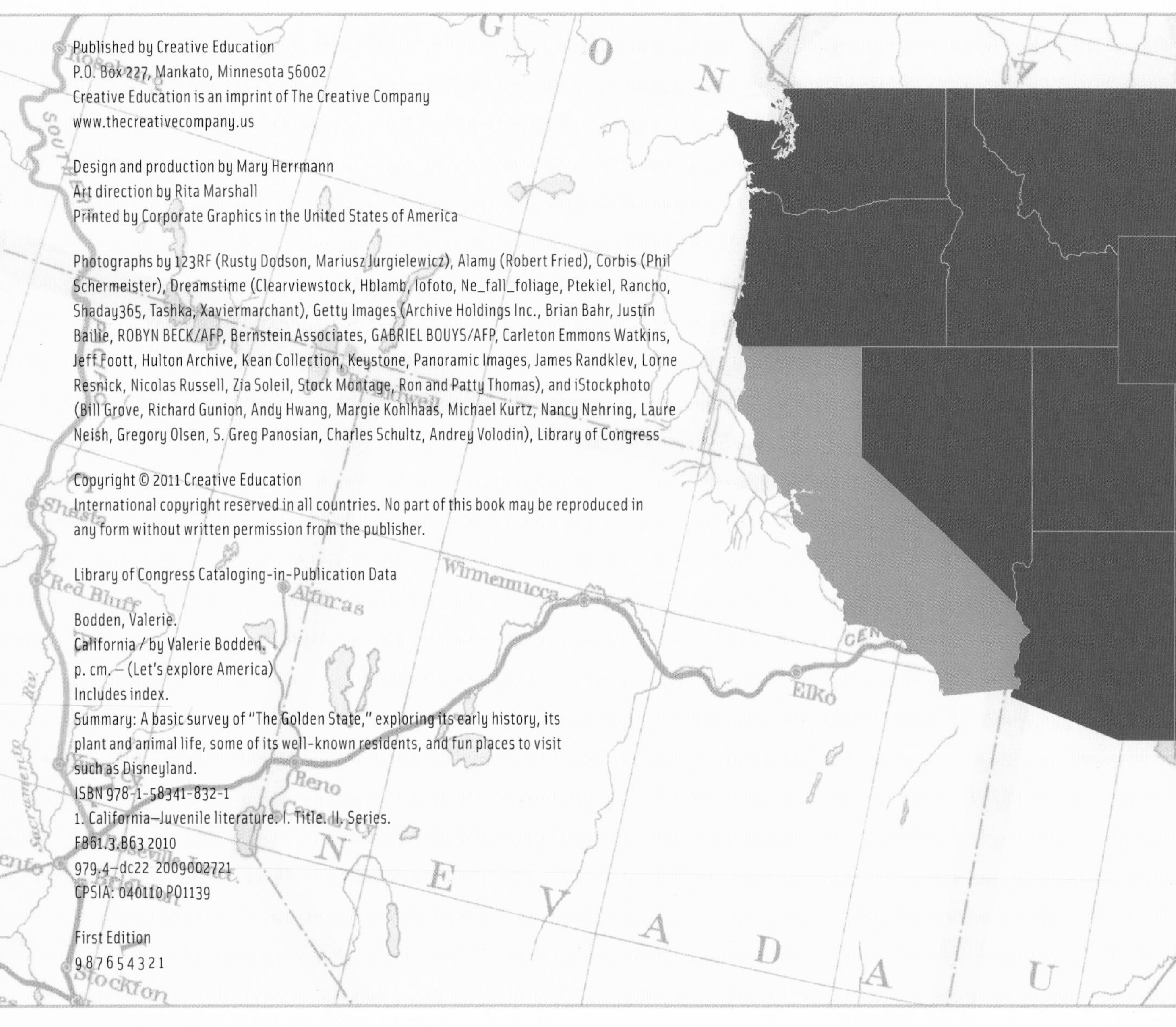

Published by Creative Education
P.O. Box 227, Mankato, Minnesota 56002
Creative Education is an imprint of The Creative Company
www.thecreativecompany.us

Design and production by Mary Herrmann
Art direction by Rita Marshall
Printed by Corporate Graphics in the United States of America

Photographs by 123RF (Rusty Dodson, Mariusz Jurgielewicz), Alamy (Robert Fried), Corbis (Phil Schermeister), Dreamstime (Clearviewstock, Hblamb, Iofoto, Ne_fall_foliage, Ptekiel, Rancho, Shaday365, Tashka, Xaviermarchant), Getty Images (Archive Holdings Inc., Brian Bahr, Justin Bailie, ROBYN BECK/AFP, Bernstein Associates, GABRIEL BOUYS/AFP, Carleton Emmons Watkins, Jeff Foott, Hulton Archive, Kean Collection, Keystone, Panoramic Images, James Randklev, Lorne Resnick, Nicolas Russell, Zia Soleil, Stock Montage, Ron and Patty Thomas), and iStockphoto (Bill Grove, Richard Gunion, Andy Hwang, Margie Kohlhaas, Michael Kurtz, Nancy Nehring, Laure Neish, Gregory Olsen, S. Greg Panosian, Charles Schultz, Andrey Volodin), Library of Congress

Copyright © 2011 Creative Education
International copyright reserved in all countries. No part of this book may be reproduced in any form without written permission from the publisher.

Library of Congress Cataloging-in-Publication Data

Bodden, Valerie.
California / by Valerie Bodden.
p. cm. – (Let's explore America)
Includes index.
Summary: A basic survey of "The Golden State," exploring its early history, its plant and animal life, some of its well-known residents, and fun places to visit such as Disneyland.
ISBN 978-1-58341-832-1
1. California—Juvenile literature. I. Title. II. Series.
F861.3.B63 2010
979.4—dc22 2009002721
CPSIA: 040110 P01139

First Edition
9 8 7 6 5 4 3 2 1

CREATIVE EDUCATION

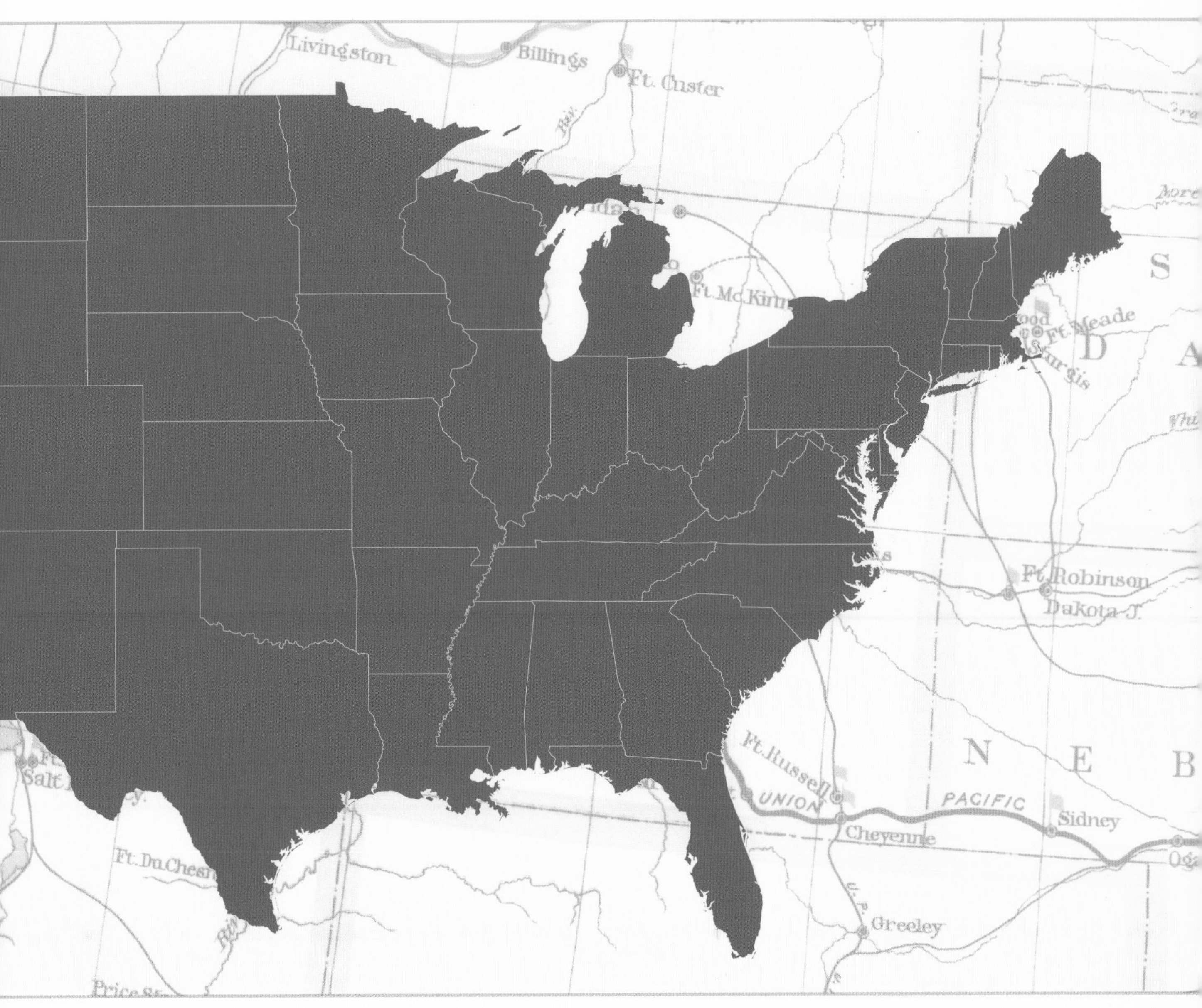
Livingston
Billings
Ft. Custer
Ft. Meade
Ft. Robinson
Dakota J.
Ft. Russell
UNION
PACIFIC
Cheyenne
Sidney
Greeley

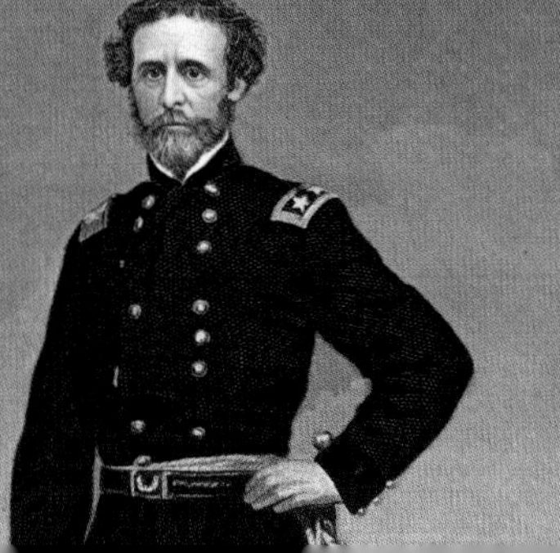

TOP, THEN LEFT TO RIGHT:

- *Men traveling to California to look for gold*
- *Captain John Fremont, who helped explore California*
- *An old California town where people used to mine for gold*
- *Gold nuggets in a mining pan*
- *Cowboys riding horses in California*

California is a state in the western part of America. It is a big state. California became a state in 1850. California is nicknamed "The Golden State." This is because people found a lot of gold there.

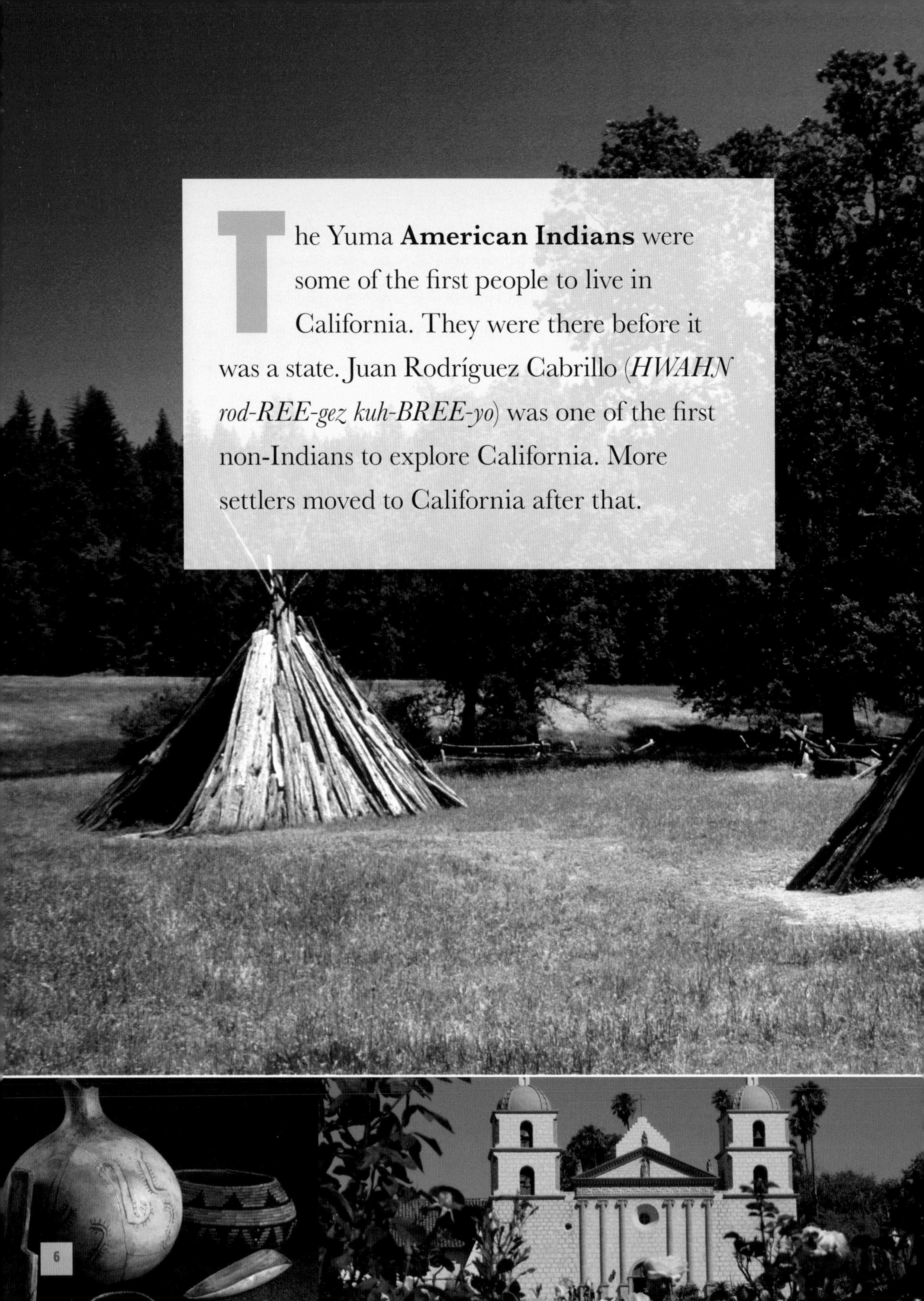

The Yuma **American Indians** were some of the first people to live in California. They were there before it was a state. Juan Rodríguez Cabrillo (*HWAHN rod-REE-gez kuh-BREE-yo*) was one of the first non-Indians to explore California. More settlers moved to California after that.

TOP, THEN LEFT TO RIGHT:

- *Shelters in California built like old American Indian homes*
- *A church built by some of the first non-Indian people in California*
- *A Yuma Man*
- *The city of San Francisco, California, in 1868*

One side of California touches the Pacific Ocean. There are many beaches there. There are forests, **mountains**, and **deserts** in California, too. California is warm in the summer. Winters are rainy or snowy in some places.

TOP, THEN LEFT TO RIGHT:

- *People on a California beach*
- *Boats in the water of the Pacific Ocean*
- *The Sierra Nevada mountains*
- *A California desert and mountains*
- *Palm trees along a California street*

Farmers in California grow tomatoes and oranges. Fir and redwood trees grow in California's forests. Elk, bears, and deer live in the forests. Coyotes and lizards live in the deserts.

TOP, THEN LEFT TO RIGHT:

- *Baskets of California tomatoes*
- *Oranges being picked*
- *A tunnel through a dead redwood tree*
- *A spiny lizard*
- *An elk in a California state park*

California's state flower is the golden poppy. The golden poppy is an orange wildflower. California's state bird is the California valley quail. The California valley quail is a gray and brown bird. California's state tree is the California redwood. The California redwood is the world's tallest tree.

TOP, THEN LEFT TO RIGHT:

- *California hills covered with poppies*
- *California valley quail*
- *A close-up view of golden poppies*
- *A forest of redwood trees*

GRAUMANS

California has more people than any other state. Some of California's people make computers. Some are farmers. Many people in California make movies.

Ronald Reagan was a famous actor who lived in California. He became the 40th president of the United States in 1981. Writer Jack London was born in California in 1876.

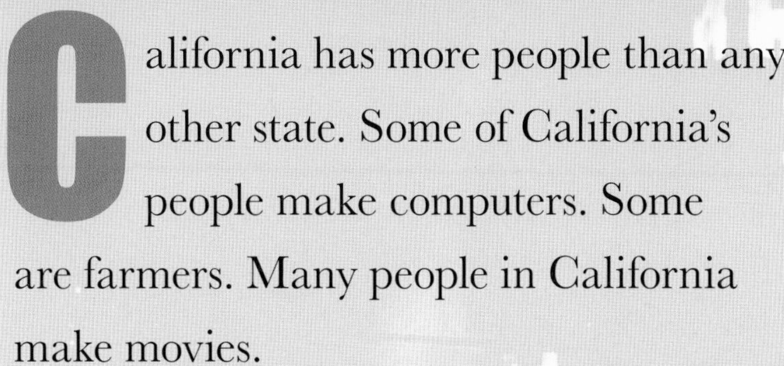

TOP, THEN LEFT TO RIGHT:

- *A street in Hollywood, California, in the 1940s*
- *A tiny computer part called a chip*
- *Ronald Reagan, when he was a young actor*
- *People using cameras to film a movie*
- *Beverly Hills, a rich city in California*
- *Writer Jack London*

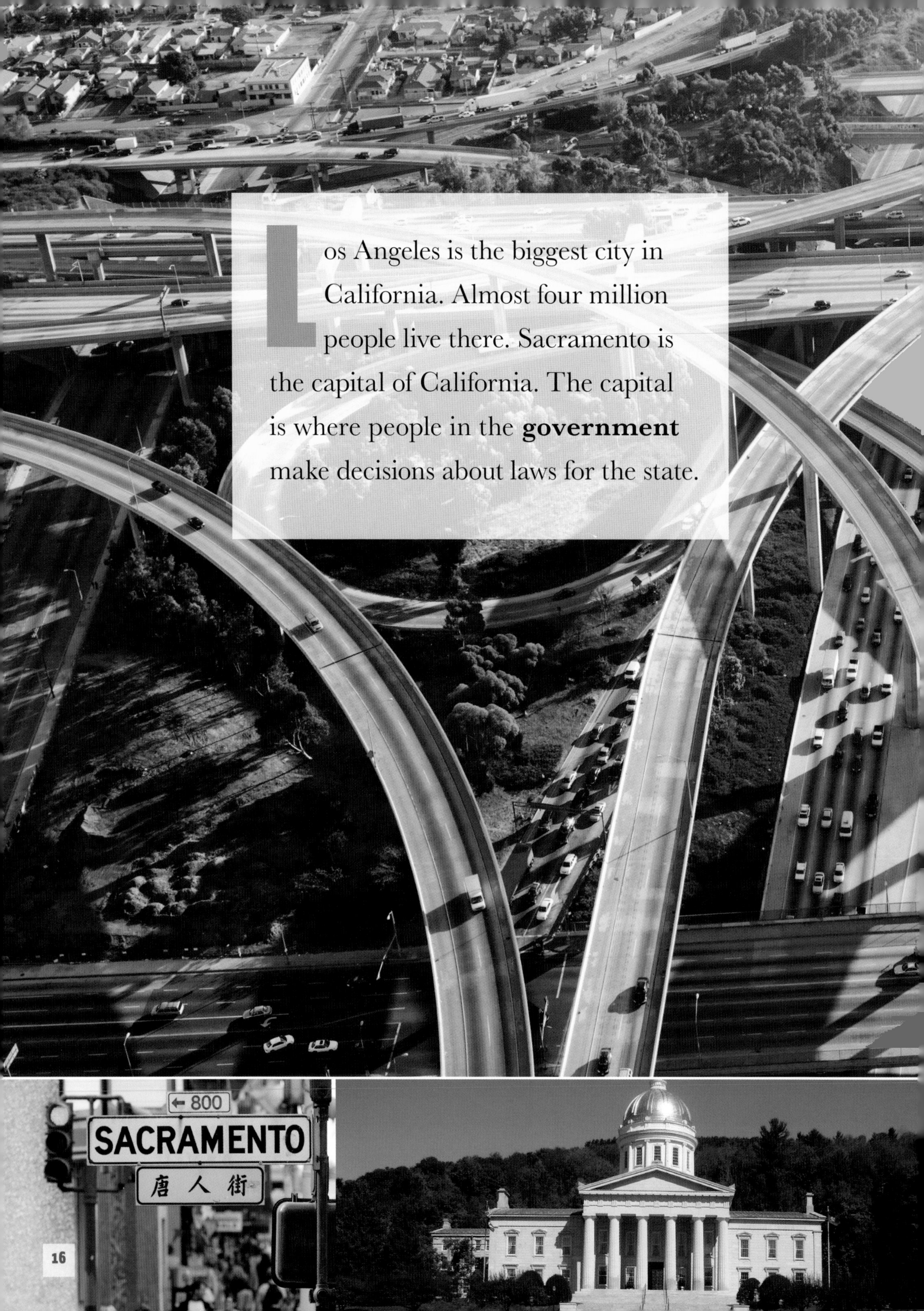

Los Angeles is the biggest city in California. Almost four million people live there. Sacramento is the capital of California. The capital is where people in the **government** make decisions about laws for the state.

TOP, THEN LEFT TO RIGHT:

- *Busy Los Angeles roads called freeways*
- *A sign for a street called Sacramento*
- *The state capitol (main government building)in Sacramento*
- *A Los Angeles Dodgers baseball player*
- *A view of Los Angeles from the sky*

Every year, lots of people visit Disneyland amusement park in California. Others go to Yosemite (*yo-SEH-muh-tee*) National Park. California has lots of fun places for everyone!

TOP, THEN LEFT TO RIGHT:

- *A ride at Disneyland*
- *People floating down a river in Yosemite National Park*
- *A skier in the California mountains*
- *A diver going into the Pacific Ocean*
- *The San Francisco 49ers football team*

FACTS ABOUT CALIFORNIA

First year as a state: *1850*

Population: *36,961,664*

Capital: *Sacramento*

Biggest city: *Los Angeles*

Nickname: *The Golden State*

State bird: *California valley quail*

State flower: *golden poppy*

State tree: *California redwood*

A pier, or big dock, on a California beach

GLOSSARY

American Indians—people who lived in America before white people arrived

deserts—big, hot areas sometimes covered with sand

government—a group that makes laws for the people of a state or country

mountains—very tall, steep hills made out of rock

READ MORE

De Capua, Sarah. *California*. New York: Children's Press, 2004.

Domeniconi, David. *G Is for Golden: A California Alphabet*. Chelsea, Mich.: Sleeping Bear Press, 2002.

LEARN MORE

Enchanted Learning: California
http://www.enchantedlearning.com/usa/states/california/index.shtml
This site has California facts, maps, and coloring pages.

Kids Konnect: California
http://www.kidskonnect.com/content/view/169/27
This site lists facts about California.

The Golden Gate Bridge
in San Francisco

A Joshua tree in the California desert

INDEX